Alan Marshfield

# The Elektra Poems

Anvil Press Poetry

Published in 1982
by Anvil Press Poetry Ltd
69 King George Street London SE10 8PX
ISBN 0 85646 085 0

Printed in Hungary

This book is published
with financial assistance from
The Arts Council of Great Britain

ACKNOWLEDGEMENTS

Some of these poems first appeared in the booklets *Dragonfly*
(Oasis Books, 1972) and *Mistress* (Anvil Press Poetry, 1972), and
in the following publications and programmes, to whose editors
acknowledgements are due: *The Listener; New Measure; New Poetry 1*
(Arts Council); *The New Statesman; Oasis; Pink Peace; Poetry Now* and
*The Poet's Voice* (BBC); the Sceptre Press broadsheets; *The Times
Literary Supplement* and *Workshop*.

# THE ELEKTRA POEMS

To darling Pod on her travels

Daddy.

# Contents

# Love Story

When the sun's in its meridian power
the pimpernel shuts. At a similar hour
your Hillman Imp bumps stop on a verge
of littered grass, onto which we emerge
hiding each from the other incitable eyes.
We leg over ruts to where dragonflies
stitch a pond's sleep, fish-plops are heard.
There are ordered elysia on the loosest word
spoken by each immodest limb.
Senses daubed upon; actions dim.
Haste alone is anathema.
What is that animal sound? The car?
No, it's switched off. It's me. Relax.

Our picnics of carefree sex offend
perhaps a cow, but we don't ask it.
Pasture and pulse should know how to mix.
The excuse for appetency's tricks
when—the plates put away and shut the basket—
a rainbow finds us at its end
is: we are summer, love is the gnats.

Resign your last stitch of repute
to the still floor uncritical of your cute
curious frailty somehow worn.
Lies do not heal what time has torn
but if they make it seem less lewd
then I will lie; your gratitude
regales me with an answer kiss.
If love is a doomed edifice
with cellars where the thick moss lingers
why should we not with festive fingers
pull it down like a warm hood
about our ears? Downfall is good
at keeping the heat in as it crumbles.

But blandly met we are very far
from smelling danger in this rose,
your oyster rose, your little flame.
Its fragrance (another's would be the same)
conduces to one night's repose,
informs of no ineluctable star
dooming the sleepy hand that fumbles.

The shadows in the garden move to night.
Draw-to your curtains, let green light,
sea-green lamplight, spoil the room.
Crush day's argument, precious gloom,
and dear dunce, blink. It amazes me
how your stupid eyes can still blissfully
illuminate, vulgarian,
this dim bed, sticky aquarium
I wallow in. I wallow in it!
Do that again. You take a minute
regarding me—it feels an hour—
and then those hands, bringing so near the sour
moment, never extinguishing. . .

Little rich girl, not so beautiful,
drown me forever in your weekend house
away from the day I do badly in.
I like it all, all, down to the swim
to those skilled-as-if-oiled hands that dowse
so well in me. The hands are all!
An hour more, then the other thing.

Nicely, heart's bawd, your words caress:
'This that thou dost, call it gentilesse,
Compassioun, felawship, and trist,'
smiling as fairly as Judas kissed:
this that I do. Tell me, whoremonger,
do ruses make innocence the younger?—
kissing my way through a social fraud,
pinning compassionate love like a gaud
to the coat that hides my jealousy.
Heart, let us practise for two or three
minutes how we may set up trust
and fellowship in this house of dust,
a stay for travellers, well adorned.

But who are these women with broken necks
that lie in rape at the foot of the stairs
divested of their expensive pearls?
O golden lads, more golden girls,
see what the heart does unawares
with its 'welcome' chalked on the house of sex.
Who more duped than these? Who more warned?

'Promise,' she said. — Although we'd said,
as a law, we'd quit when the thing was dead;
—hadn't I given a giftshop lark
of spindle glass, which in the park
we'd rubbed in mud one autumn evening
where fed-up parakeets were preening
and said, this screwy lark is us?
It's cheap, it doesn't make a fuss.
We'll say it sings—for love of the thing;
though I cannot promise it will always sing
like this. 'Promise,' she said. — And I saw
how it was with her. Neither our 'law'
nor the song I mentioned affected her.
'That we'll always be happy.' Her small hands were
(those hands!) white. Her eyes were pain.

Silent, Compassion entered my head
and the Comradeship I hadn't earned
and a decent type called Civility
and Trust with its charge of apostasy
to return their verdict, and I turned
to let her know. 'I promise,' I said,
'to show you the bird when it sings again.'

Love, perhaps? Perhaps I loved.
I used to like the way we roughed
it in so many beds. Her talk
of high-class whoring, the lack of sulk,
I liked all that. But when I left
there was (and it hurt) a specially deft
touch that remained. There was a thing
about her voice. She throated spring
before the birds had drowsily thought
of it. How deeply well she caught
that hollow pitch the sun had yet
to fill; then she poured in; her debt
to Italian ancestors, that sound.

I spoke the voice of colder sires.
My home spur, poor hill, hated her.
Yet I grant all hills, near or far,
but apologetic orchestra
for her, their scraggy nymph, to stir
with her gifted hand, to the breath of the choirs
of angelic putti that clasp her round.

'Oh bloody hills, darker and vaster,
will nothing go from my loose mind? Last year
I had this man in my car came riding
every week to the lake, confiding
his claptrap of "What's best, loves
and then buries its love in leaves."
He put it on my pillow in his goodbye note.
I've had it before. He even wrote
"What is the use of memory and
despair? Eat people with your hand,
your delicate lust, your dirty soul,
and then forget them." That—to console!
My people-eating so in arrears.

'Then this lark came out of my house, to see
a rich bitch scratch at the autumn sky,
"Promise me," calling, "that I'll forget!"
"The dry leaf is very soon wet, unwet,"
said he, cocking his glassy eye.
I cried and went out shakily
to be eaten again, to find volunteers.'

# Sleep, Silhouette

Sleep, silhouette, beneath night's bridge
in a gown of water. My voice I give,
weak with insistence, to the sharp air;
the key is taken by those xylophone lights
that dint the black ebb we are lapped in.
Still world. What do I ask for? Names
for what we are, our deeps perform.
Cold shadow, sleep now, one day's love
having drained us with sweet tribulation.
We know of pangs, for bodies feel
but only the mind remembers. Slide
into this numb death of satiety,
a forced integument of clammy rest,
green lips apart, I with no name
to designate our effort and our loss.

A tide, but not of sleep, steals you.
Behind the dear brown of your eye's gristle
I hear the enchantment of bruised sobs.
I know the pain. Rehearse me while I live.
Recall, moist bulletin, my tongue.
And my ambassador fingers grown aware
liquidity means use, meant readiness.
I was not marginal; dealt close—
scorning your prelude whimper—stung
your red interior with singing pains,
longer joys scattering then, until
from crotch to chin our sweaty bodies held
and we arrived, gyrating breast to breast,
at motion like the motion of a stone
wherein we learned duration, beyond grief.

We were not satisfied. Who is, alive?
The human fascinated. We forsook
the mood of granite; eddied to brinks,

testing disintegration till we fell,
being weary of stone, for only flesh keeps time.
Rested. Resumed. And the day died.
A cold wind came and still no name
for the scared sorrows lapping our arched bones.
No name. An eye—no name—behind the moon
explores me with your stare, that's all.

Until I know. Your arms: in them
I have shown mercy to the egregious moon,
to the pathetic stars and to my flesh.
Now like a boom a recognition breathes.
I've found content more final than a name.
Upon your lids darkens the bruise of sorrow.
Sleep hardens our insoluble lives.
Lights die. But the world's over now.

# It Smells of Mortality

Not civet's ooze nor *Magie* by Lancôme
hangs particles of much-desired scent
in my olfactory entrances.
Should they invade, my nostril's flair rebel!
Snort them away, usher them out, them all:
the farding stills of Grasse may tickle some
        but leave me cold as stone

I find synthetics thin, and if I must
absorb the oils of more exquisite vats,
quaffing lewd stinks cured into fragrancy,
I'll only take them, atomised and rare,
so long as some of the lewd tang is there,
redolent of bitch urine or field crust
        or may-bush petalled with flies.

But better than such bottled sex-spore is
the trace my love leaves where she's laid her down.
The way I make my sense dilate
is drubbing it with odours of the pore,
the body's slag and unhygienic ore
exuded from dark pits. All these I kiss
        and she is not offended.

The ripe warehouse knows my dependency
and I have lurked about the mature farms.
But most of all, my dear, I say
the freighted odours with which I collide
in cobbled markets or the rank seaside
reduce me less than your crammed pungency,
        your punnets of aroma.

If love is a singing fish in a wicker creel
much used and salt, and curious to the nose,
it's not its death but dying smells.
I, mandarin, perceive its air not thin
but dyed with our mortality, dear kin;
and I gloat that I have some sense to feel
                    how much life's in decay.

# Aries

He must destroy what has destroyed
so much, lop out what has annoyed
the swart flesh of his race too long:
the thieves of dignity; the pale
dredgers of muck whose suck and sale
of lives still saps like dysentery;
the farmer, prig and missionary;
the special squads that come around.
What he now forges underground,
self-payment for what else he's mined,
is a weapon kissing-keen to find
its thwarted consummation's cue.
Then ram will tup with the white ewe;
the marriage yield a bloody wife.

Wishful to think that he might make
honourably at least his black
and disproportionate demand.
When anger and fear provoke his hand
it is unlikely he will think to hack
with fierce compassionate care, and slake
the bayonet as if a surgeon's knife.

# Rye

For the moment the thin tea and the floury scones
until the rain pulls off, then we'll expend
the rest of our ambition on the town,
digest the streets down to their cobbled spines,
nibble the scallops on the rectory styles
and top off with the evening's salad air.

And there's a woman tidying our wrack
both in the tearooms and the town we leave,
her starched white figure raking industriously
the paper napkins and the dusk of streets,
nursing the debris of our appetites:
the mummy who forgives us our small greed.

# A Child Waking

*for Undine*

Unoccupied by sleep the infant cries.
She tries a mew until it's a miaow
that rises through the cot-rails, silent bars,
sharp-edged, to where it's recognised.

Like two boarders, poised, upside down, mother
is there, father; they take her up.
In her cheek is pressed a whisper, which is wet.
Her eyes look round; she hears articles hover.

The clock slots into the moonlight on the sill.
The night clouds in their usual aquarium
look through black brittle trees. Nearer, a nose
rests among shadows; its temperature is nil.

Above it a forehead exists in the known
dark of father. Dark mother's lips
play busily and subdue. As might subdue
a homesick girl mere promise of going home.

She is returned, tucked in. The bluey bits
of parents are there, watching, and then not there.
She wants to cry. And would. Except that sleep
finds just the space of darkness, and she fits.

# The Birth of Venus

I, lame god, hide, muttering in my teeth,
stuck in this cliff-hole of an executive suite
where fingers peck typewriters; tide-streams beneath
of taxis and malcontents lick, seethe and bleat.

Waiting for her to be born, my Venus, bride.
What rescue from the glassplate grim forge of London?
A vapouring where boil my sight lines, where fried
car tops gleam frolicsomely, car-fumes wanton.

Till she, my lovely, my lot, clears the light-pools
(hair and head). My manic eyes are cones
that twinge and flip me out of my spectacles
and I'm down there, *Volcanus furens*, on the stones.

Her eyes are as empty and smiling as the future,
her hair fresh yellow round her mignonne head.
Neck gracile and pouting mouth. Nature
delivers to me from the ocean bed

the target of the whole world's erotic itch:
beauty of flesh, flesh soft, perfect harmony,
yet spoiling with the quirks of change and the rich
varieties of love. Mine, but I see

to every lording jack how she is cheap,
from martial bigshot, planning his push-stud war,
to that gravity who bares her in his sleep—
the mortal father of Rome—she plays the whore...

The waves, the very waves, are tantalised,
the glinting evil of steel. She's Mecca and ease
to the search of all the bifurcated lives
that ache to be lost, pleasured in striptease.

With tripping breasts and with a waist so small
it makes the nostrils flare, abundant thigh
and long legs of the fleeting animal:
how could she not be butt to every eye,

making men jocular about their lust?
She is a honey slander cannot mar.
(Ink's got into my nails, they seem to rust,
and men are laughing in the public bar.)

Only I fully know her. Cuckold. Lame.
Work-bent each day until my muscles crack.
Powerless, hideous, pious. Only I can tame
that sea-born body struggling to get back.

# The Evil Secateurs

Prometheus, steal me a rose.
I don't care what your brother says.
Steal it.

Old sloppy, happy Epi, who condones
a side of beef but not the thighs of girls:
kowtow not to him, friend.

Take out your evil secateurs
and snip me that
aculeate, metallic

rose.
I have immortal longings to consume
that pinky lettuce poll.

I have observed
how at the clack and rictus of that flower
the Sunday citizens all shy away.

So I would have it, must commune
with that fierce thing that is so foli ite
yet hides its heart.

Its heart. Its heart.
I'll eat it to the heart.
And I'll be filled with such a turbulent calm

as neither muck nor amethyst will faze.
And let the bought priests lie
about our punishment.

The gods will give long life
to us who love them so.
So now. The rose!

# Feel Good

In my garden fluff-heads and bald eyes
of dandelions stand high:
they have to, the grass is deep.

In my garden I have spies
in the periscoped butterflies
while I lie naked.

In my garden I feel good.
Buttercup and charlock stand two foot.
No prim daisy by my side.

Dates will drop from the dock leaves
and aphids give me milk
as I grow big and cool.

Soon the grass will be more.
It will hide the house next door.

# My Death Began

### I

Last night, like a new cause, my death began.
I met the past, the days ahead without me.

Began as I stalked through the pass of love.
I saw my leaving. Not as it once was: hook!

Hook that was parting from another love
when I made the day's deeds medallions.

'Fish do not feel,' that other love had said.
Fish flesh a bag; hook-wrench; drift light at sea.

### II

That first love made my mind a trap for fear.
Last night I had no fear. I said, 'I die.'

My first love taught me: look, the end of us
is pain, a tearing. Love me. Nothingness.

But nothing is, my love last night told me,
mere hole between the worlds that we define.

Feel round those holes, feel elbow-deep round them.
My time was up: I touched the worlds around.

Eating my bread in secret, I communed
with weak-back men, slack women of the plain;

with Macedonian bloods like lekking cocks,
louche orgies, wars and work, the sea around.

III

Such things the bedside light told, and I looked
down at a heap of dank and squeaking bones,

her breasts, abdomen, that are now so neat,
I saw pushed to one side, chewed chicken, gone.

I paddled in the going, while I held
the unrecognisable other from the tomb.

I saw her future with no jealousy.
I felt my death begin. I had begun.

# Thanatos

*for Lise*

On Lago di Garda: a time to collect thoughts
and renew love. All morning under my ear
the lure of water clonks through the dark
in the lonely lilo on which I ride,
bronzed by a tourist sun, arms sunk in cool,
a fugitive, an unnorthed compass pin,
idle inside the closed eyes' hatch of red.
Far cry of bathers scribbles on my ear
like mobilising nerves a war away.
I turn and stare across the hot wide lake
and look up valleys, it seems, fifty miles.

Clothed in crease from new duck pants to smile,
I strut night streets,
follow the echo of a dark I have,
drifting through postcard streets
in Bardolino to the lakeside quay.
I watch the sunset peel its orange in
the dying sea. The lovers, white,
sit and take coffee with the scene.
From far away the valley unseen pours
its pricks of light in a great Nile of dark
foreclosing in that dark the dark
soft silt of pledge in cups.
And another day without you is nearly gone.

# Eros

That puzzled mouth. I remember
how a year ago on this same bed
I was relieved as you expelled our child.
Your throat sucked up and bit the air and made it
scream for its life while I crooned to you.
Now again your body is rising angrily
crying incontinent in the throes of love
that the day be burst, the supplicant panting
interesting me as if I were outside,
a surgeon, listening.
                And I have both times
been at sea. From a gulf-tempest comes
the noise of living hulks breaking like pods
and that fierce cause, the sympathetic sea,
intoning as its wrecks explode ashore.
May I make similar sounds at all your labours.

# Genesis at Up Marden

Behind the barn, half-barn-size and half-seen
between yew crops, it stands low in its graves.
   Stone cherubs, blind with time's gangrene,
struggle to feed to bones earth still depraves
      with nervous roots and slimes
      the Hampshire scene, the well-heeled lane
      contenting beefy families still.
Over the cringing dead behind the times:
Up Marden church—the charged and empty Will.

The dead behind you, enter in and be
chilled by the frugal origin of air,
      encounter an ancient poverty
that cannot impress, not even self-aware,
        just nondescript. The pews
      are scruffy, but for two or three
      minutes now are comfort enough,
while a winter hiker scrapes mud from his shoes,
to savour the absence in of mind and love.

Bells in the clapboard tower have inspired
a trickle across the centuries from the race
      of cowman and navy man retired
to kneel in this bare and undistinguished plaee.
      Though why they trod so far
      is queer, unless some nothing called
      to tell how proto-reason planned
a ball of mud and flame near a faint star
to howl through space, become a fibrous gland

as pain took root. The clog of the bright share
gravels the Will, whose dereliction wrecks
      the midshipman malaria
licked far from home. The strident nerves make, flex
      of cruel, self-wounding arms,

the bare Will lacerate and grow
in ever-changing glamour. Puce
quarrels of wood, glissando scarp, fat farms,
beget in the tiny soul moods less obtuse—

for whom no priest can come now on his calls.
The sleek irrelevant hands will not annoy
        with pan the uncollected falls
of dust behind the font. Stiff chains deploy
        four candelabra, slight
        convex serrated squares of brass
        like eggshell Frankish crowns, askew
from whitewashed beams. From these have come the light,
gleams in the emptiness, gleams mean and few.

This is the very first place. Here retire
when you have switched synapses to the mind
        and gauged the fare of flame and mire.
This is where life starts, empty-handed, blind,
        different from us, a snake
        of rhythmic spaces, unaware.
        Space has its own laws. At their core
there is the Will to matter, the Will to wake
itself, a creeping Will, pigheaded, poor.

Upon the altar there are honesty leaves,
thin as rice-paper, excellent and dead,
        and then an Armistice poppy that achieves
its purpose in that it recalls the bed
        of bones beneath this hole
        that breed vermiculated caves
        in the dank air of a scullery,
the work-bare, skrimshank, first yawn of the soul
from which time flits away each century.

This air is death's too. Dead, the bones behind,
you only are aware by being seen.
        Time is the soul you die to find

and you have died already. The thwart green
of downs is where your doubt
took root and voyages were planned.
Tell it the dead again. Your jaws
relay it better than the stone. Speak out
and hear in this tunnel the faint first applause.

# Dragonfly

I am a god, a membranous whirl, a powerful thruster, brilliant, whose origin is the Nile. I am a foe of the landlogged, of those wizened by angers.

I emerge one night from a dead skin with new wings to glisten in the moon and shall live for a summer.

Down in the water, waterlogged, I admit it, I struggle for steps not there, in ridiculous drag, snapped at by fish not big enough for my skin, and I get somehow out on a rope's end.

Hovering like a module sliding backwards and forth, visible stay of invisible piston, oiled with the blue of the air, I am purposeful search and explorer in need of supplies.

Carnivorous and predacious, patrolling a beat, devourer daily of many times my own weight, I have powerful jaws and dismember prey on the wing.

I zoom in like an ancient biplane laden with bombs to accrete like stately vol-au-vents in the leprous drawing rooms, in the concentrations of death.

In the sloping life-support system of my thorax are medicaments to meet every imagined contingency. I can change your mind at a moment's notice. I am the funny wizard. You need not beware.

I have, if you like, a mission. Who has not? At Copenhagen, docked, I register a lighthouse island approachable only by hydroplane. There the heroines stayed: Cleopatra, Florence Nightingale and Modesty Blaise.

I take each in turn and I hold her neck with my knees and we mate like that. She washes her eggs off to look after themselves. The nymphs will take three years to moult to size in the ooze.

My whole head is encased in the great helmeted eyes composed of a thousand facets. My knowledge is a mosaic of light and movement.

I look in the dish of each flower that is busily recording pulsars and electrical storms on the sun. I note its spectra and function and style— and my categories are enlarged.

I dart sideways by disappearing and appearing again five years away to the left in the same instant.

Sheering in past Tilbury over the cancered pelvis of England, rubbled with daisies and rusty boilers, I descend, a serious animal, an analogy fighting analogy, looking for a mate and a prey before I dispatch to die very soon in the ice at the pole.

# Charm

Against catastrophe. Take Wild Angelica, Truelove, Summerlocks,
Sweethearts, Sungreen and Traveller's Ease. Chop fine,
hash with Kisses and Keys of Heaven, Lady-never-fade and Lily-royal.
Leave them to dry in memory's sun, along with Chitchat,
Confetti and Baby's Rattle. Add water and simmer with
Morning Glory, My Lady's Lace, Bunny Rabbit and Sleepyhead.
Then, biting your lip, fling Spindlewood in, Love-links, Snow Toss,
    Cuckold.
Tasting blood, mash in with White Robin and Remember-me.

But perhaps the evil has happened. Go in then for
more vicious weeds. Find Adder's Spit, Snaggs and Strangleweed,
blending with Blood Cup, Toad's Head, Tormentil. Seethe in
    snake's oil
with Sheep Rot, Poison More, Hacks, Earthgall, Devil's Guts
and Death Come Quickly. Thicken to a broth.
Add Fellonwort, Moonog and Bad Man's Bread.
When this coagulates sprinkle the skin
with Bitchwood, Bastard Killer and Mad Woman's Milk.
This should finish your harassers, he and she, but if
they still thrive, pick yourself up, make the following dram:

Get Sod-apple, Bog Hop, Sow's Tits, Bladders of Lard,
Hypocrite, Mare-fart and Devil May Care. That's a beginning.
Set about a truly baroque cauldron. Take Naked Virgins
and Naughty Man's Plaything. Pick Flirtweed, Meg Many Feet,
Kitty-come-down-the-garden-lane-jump-up-and-kiss-me,
Slags, Boots and Stockings, Sucky Sue and Stinking Jenny.
Stir in grosser weeds. Add Dirty Dick, Bull's Bags,
Little Peeper, Jack-jump-about. Make these work upon
Maiden's Heads, Tiger's Mouth, Open and Shut,
Thunder Cup, Water Squirt and Tittle-my-fancy.
If your pain is strong there are other simples: Broomrape,
Jack-o'-both-sides, Rawheads and Rantipole.
By now you should feel better. You can finish the spell with

34

Publicans, Bottle and Drunken Willy; Bellywind, Pisspot,
Welcome-home-husband-though-never-so-drunk,
Cat Bed and Alleluiah. But if your ache is persistent
and jealousy grinds against desolation,
infuse then a cup of Dead Man's Grief, swallow it down,
lie down your last amid Cuckoo's Sorrow
under a draughty Dogberry Tree.

# Queen Tiye

White wife of scoured stone, a bloodless scar
at your brows' lobe: my shrivelling eyes
will never turn you from the high probe
your eyes wear. You focus on the far
far inside you. What you intend is
your horizon. It inflates your lips
with a dry smile. Sunlight bleaches you
and makes you more inevitable.
Possession of you acids my touch.
My arteries wither. Crook and flail
are my kingly weapons, they suffice
a king. Dark in the lunar fields
that you erect with phosphorus corn
I wait and, with a sun-slash, slash them
into my grain bin. Wife, why are you
troubled? Is it the death I bear? See?
That no more moves you than pain or waste.
Brutality's emissary, I
donate the marts I gain, the power.
While what you see turning in your head's
mercurial spaces you project
into stalks, stars and inundation.
So why that vexed jot between your eyes?
Is it a human relic? I'd thought
you had stirred so deeply through your courts
into cells of superconsciousness
where life throbs, that you were wholly sane.
Do you, down your isolation's bore,
blink at a lanky girl half turning,
turning but never gone? Queen Tiye,
let it be my slurred lot to mourn her,
I, the sun that dies. Shrink if you must
into your palace. Grind the dark with
its cold doors. But do not close your eyes.

# Ta-hes Visits Her Tomb

Let us go to the necropolis
for a good read. Qaha is graining
the last chunk for my mausoleum.
Soon, children, he will be inserting
the east slab on which my life will go.
Though that won't be till I go. I'll not
have those coarse masons take their rubbings
of my scratch for the scribes, yet. Varnish
those eyes with oil, my scrawny liebchen.
That sand has more disaster in it
than all the Seth of Lower Egypt.

Leapfrog down to the last mastaba?
If you must. But don't forget I'm here.
So this is it. Blank epitaph. What
relief carved there would best betray me,
hue and cry, seeking a vent to life?
Something curt, witty, uncertain. Here,
perhaps, my self's familiar. With Bes,
guard of bed and belly, ugly, old
fat nurse, bringing suet or something.
And pregnant Taueret, hippo god.
Shall I again proliferate where
Osiris's Field of Rushes shows?
Please Maat, let me. You say to us: fire
shrivels. And day blurs waterblossoms.
Lady Maat, truth, let me. I'll go mad
if they won't permit me to bring forth.
Even lettuce in a garden, figs.
Or let me enter the great Nile silt,
though that is presuming, with Isis
claiming the best mud for her anxious
fibres. Besides, isn't that fancy
they have down there of weighing the heart
a bit, well? With Dog-chops at the scales

making sure the heart sinks like a bone
against the feather, Truth. As if truth
were a thing as fragile, dry as that.
I'll have a shabti dummy of me
to suffer that insult. Sacred cat!
How dare they try to measure the heart
that knows more than these hack fabulists
elaborating hieratic stills
have half the brain for! If it's reason
they're in need of, if they want to tell
how it is, how it might come to be,
they don't need gelded decretal gods
(pardon Osiris) to explain, like
Anubis with his butcher's steelyard.
For legend, let there. . . But that mural
must tender a style that's true to me
to ricochet through the flesh to come.
Depict me, Qaha, marking the dawn
past shipwrights and sextons lopping ox,
reapers, donkeys, serfs hurrying back
with kohl for madam's steatite jar,
stroppy apprentices, fishermen.
Remind me of Khnumhetep's party
in the marshes. Mother of Horus,
after the fowl in the marsh dawn! Ra!
he was so handsome. I saw him once
knock down a mallard from twenty yards
with his bent cudgel. And then that day
he had me, with Qar up at Karnak
at the assizes. Bes, what a flood
as he met me like a bearded god
with lilies round his eyes. A mantra
that was. And my Mahu has his mouth.
My son. One day you'll be chief bowman,
nomarch, the wardrobe's overseer.
You have had your start. From twenty yards!
The prodigies that Qar spawned on me
won't make the grade. Qar, my honoured judge,

38

I suppose I never expected
much husband of you. I realise
a kind of life emerges from you
as you steer appeals through sanity
to some correct end. You who control
the empire that Tuthmosis dished us,
and your museum of cronies. They
are a bright division! Running mates
of crooks, gerrymanderers, prelates
born with dialectic of the bone.
You shed light, Qar, in your way, I know.
But night comes. And will they weigh the heart?
Can you weigh loneliness, too much joy,
the bird shrieking on the starry spate,
the mind's scorpion that wants to be
a crocodile, the fertility
of the mind that wishes to embalm
more than a pulled corpse parcelled in rags,
mind that wants the self, wing'd Ba, prepared
for departure down its own dark Nile?
Heart assists. They would not weigh the heart.
My heart of different forms, do not
stand up against me as a witness,
nor make opposition against me
among the assessors. Do not weigh
heavy against me in the presence
of the balance-ward. You are only
the bludgeon that is in my body,
the creator that maintains me. I
am more than you, ever, or your whims.
I have watched you, I have played along
because the Ra that channels you must
mean something. But I have kept my self
apart. Self means more than the great sun
intends. The sun is always dying.
The self grows. Or so Wah taught me. Tomb,
depict me as a child, nubile but full
of push enough to enter into

the sidestall play as I slink at dawn
where goldsmiths grill eggs and weavers sweep,
where seamy peasants hike to work, where
swims out of the morning's cool desert
the long slow-motion tribute column
from Nubia; as I walk at dawn
past limbering prophets, scaffolding,
and kidneys frying in the sharp air.
Depict me, tomb, entering the Now
that makes the future bigger. Even
dull Qar knows. You would not weigh the heart.
Tomb picture, ritualise for me
a harvest or a winter banquet
where these governors, chancellors, priests,
recall how their thus-and-thus faltered
(to Seth with Tuthmosis and his hordes!),
learning to tambourines, harps, sistra,
what inflexions of the bloody soul
search from my carelessness and do well.
Qar, my dear husband, yes, I love you,
smell the scent that trickles from my hair,
let my henna nails gouge your smooth arm,
my pumiced lip gobble in your ear
like the night's flotsam by the hard stairs,
and let my pleated gown remind you.
Of course you like them, the topless girls,
serving the exotica of Punt.
They are hotter than baboons. Life's not
flask and pomegranate all the time,
but long enough. Qar. Come, don't fool me,
I'd sooner swallow a gekko whole
than your late-night pillow lies. I know
what happens at the Double Ibis.
We have different needs. You act on
active impulse. While I fold small things
in a chest as if for a new groom.
We move from different directions
to the pane where we're death's hesitant

reflections. You are important now.
You'll have your name up in cartouches.
God's hallowed wives and their flint dildos!
Do I care how you exert yourself?
Be brave as Anhur, thug as a fish,
what does it matter so long as you
meet your own image where I'll meet mine
and we cross each other? May Ra's eye
weep blessings through his obsidian
contact lenses. Nothing is surer
than a phylactery's frailty
against this seething sand. Does he hear?
What kind of stone? What plea? Nothing like
Thaa-em-hetep's, poor neurotic bitch,
praying to seven devils at once.
Imagine them, sneering from their cold:
'Come then, make us an offering, Thaa!'
At least, clapped down full of pious fears,
she had the salt to warn her brother
what an ugly defile tamped her tomb.
Children, that's a canopic jar. No!
There's someone's liver there, he'll wonder
where his guts have gone, or why it is
his solar disc is slipping. Still, it
no doubt pleasured him to mind his lights.
Perhaps they led him to his own life
if he wished to follow them below.

Memorial, say I was a cow
like Hathor, and wished to suckle kings.

# Leaving

A juvenile thing it is, to be told in an attic
that the weather cannot last, because it has.
There has been no summer like it. My daughter and I
prepare for the boat. She packs a spade
and tells me it cannot last. Each year the house
grows, and grows more devices: white
wooden summer villa raised out of stones.

From verandah to shore
we freight the wet heat of our bodies down—
mosquitoes, careless of life, sting
our elbows and ankles. She takes up the stern
to watch where I row, avoiding
the small rock, a nipple, pricking the water.
Gazing ahead, she sees water,
a lattice of light, and the otherside shore, forgetting
weathers don't last. I face my shore:
a pine worn red, a house disappearing
like a well-bred smile going out one summer,
out of a life, because it has to.

# Centaurs

I remember many a time when lust
roared in like centaurs. If there was one place
where life still picnicked childishly and nude
then we would find it. Thunder round a rock
like a posse of huns into that spread of limbs
of innocent outing. Scatter their braziers, winecrocks,
fruit, and tread the juice out of their males.
Just one armful of their bare rhythmic softness,
just one whiff of their frightened and thrilled sweat,
and we became destruction's seed, our brains
night-time forests and a murder of crows.
By waist or hair, arm or haunch we dragged them.
Their fear inflamed us and was their undoing,
and later, on the lake's far side, their sobs
held us to their breasts with after-kisses
and left us more four-footed than before.
But darling, there have been times, certain times,
when we have been two centaurs from the start
and all night's forest screams were waterfalls.

# Cynthia Victrix

*from Propertius*

Something tonight has scared the paludal Esquiline;
    the neighbourhood ran amok through the New Fields.
Lanuvium's tutelar presence is an ancient serpent—
    a rare hour loitering there will not be wasted.
There a sacred descent is torn down a dark gully
    where offerings come to the scrawny-gutted snake
(virgins, beware such tracks) when he claims his annual
    food-tribute, wrenching his hiss from earth's insides.
Girls sent down to these sacraments turn anaemic when
    their rash hand entrusts itself between his fangs.
Whatever titbit the virgin pokes at him he snatches
    and the basket jitters in the virgin's hand.
If they've been chaste they'll return, hugging their parents' necks,
    and the farmers cry, 'It'll be a good year now.'
To this place my Cynthia was led by tonsured ponies,
    respecting Juno—she should have said for Venus.
Tell me, Appian Way, how much triumph, to your knowledge,
    she drove in, splattering her wheels along your cobbles?
Then an ugly punch-up in a furtive bar got noisy—
    I wasn't hurt, but my reputation was.
She was a marvellous sight as she crouched across the shaft-butts,
    daring to give rein through the dirty slums.
Though I'll not detail the equipage, the Molossian dogs,
    and the Chinese silks of that creep she had in tow.
Soon he will sell his future for a vile circus feed
    when a shameful beard smudges his pampered cheeks.
And it was because she had so often wronged our bed
    I made up my mind to strike tent and couch elsewhere.
There's a Phyllis along the Aventine near Dian's temple—
    I don't like her sober: drunk, she's fanciable.
And there's Teia: she lives by the Tarpeian sacred clearing;
    she's a blonde, and slewed, one lover's not enough.
They would soothe the night away. I made a stand: invite them,
    and renovate my affairs with some untried tricks.

There was a bunk for three on a secluded lawn.
Do you ask how we had it off? I lay between.
A service of glass for the summer, Lygdamus at ladle,
and the Methymnaean taste of neat Greek wine.
An Egyptian flute-player! Castanets, Phyllis twisting—
no make-up but pretty, pleased to have a rose tossed!
And Magnus himself, with short arms, truncated legs,
clapping his maimed hands to the boxwood flute.
But the flame was unsteady from the lamp, though filled with oil,
and the tray fell face-down on its pedestal.
While I rooted for sixes from the next dice and the next
the losing singles kept on bumping out.
They bared their tits, I was blind; they sang, but I was deaf;
at Lanuvium's gates, indeed, I stood alone.
Then suddenly a door-hinge grated, and a murmur
was made in the forecourt of my sacred home!
Suddenly, Cynthia! Both doors were flung against the wall:
her hair uncared for, becoming in her frenzy.
My fingers loosened, let the goblet in them fall;
my lips, though eased with wine, lost all their red.
Her eyes electric, she lashed out with all the woman in her—
no less a spectacle than a sacked city.
Her angry fingernails lacerated Phyllis' face;
scared Teia shrieked across the near canals . . .
Lifted torches disturbed the groggy citizens
and every footway rang with the loud night.
They were swallowed by the first pub in that shady sidestreet,
their blouses undone, their hairstyles torn to rags.
Cynthia, victrix, pleased with these shreds of war, returned,
bruising my face perversely with her palm,
inflicting on my neck her mark, biting the blood out,
and above all making my eyes jog—they'd deserved it.
When pummelling me had tired her, she jerked out Lygdamus,
who was to the left somewhere, hiding under
the bed. Exposed, he called on my protecting geist:
Lygdamus, I was useless—captured too.
At last, with supplicatory hands, I met her terms,
though she'd scarcely show her foot for me to hold.

She said: 'If you want me to overlook your little faults,
    hear what the format of my law's to be.
Never stroll about in Pompey's arcade at your best,
    nor in the lecherous Forum when the sand's strewn.
Don't twist your neck, at the play, to gawk at the top circle;
    and when a litter's unveiled, don't lurk around.
Above all, let the whole cause of my sorrow, Lygdamus,
    be sold, and drag from his feet a brace of chains.'
And so she laid down her law. 'I will stick to it,' I said.
    She laughed, elated with the power I'd given.
Then she fumigated with scent each place the other girls
    had touched, and washed down the doorstep with clear water.
She ordered me to change into other outdoor clothes
    and touched my head three times with burning sulphur;
and when every sheet on the mattress had been changed too,
                          [I matched her:
    we sheathed the sword on the familiar bed.

# Cynthia Restored

*from Propertius*

The Spirits do exist. Death's never the end of us.
The fires of cremation baffled, the pale ghost escapes.
For Cynthia came, a vision, inclining across my pillow—
lately interred in the brouhaha of the roadside—
to see the poor insomniac, lately from love's wake come,
racked that the sheets that were once his estate were cold.
It was still the same, her hair, as it was at her funeral;
her eyes the same; and the cloth at her side was charred.
The fire had eaten the beryl ring that was on her finger,
and her lips were chapped with the surface waters of Lethe.
Both were alive: the voice coming from her, the understanding;
but on her hand a splintery thumb-bone rattled.

'You bastard, though one couldn't have hoped for a better man...
Can sleep get to work so soon, when I'm hardly cold?
Our sleepless intrigues in the Subura erased so early?
And the sill our nocturnal tactics had worn away,
which I threw a rope from so often, dangling from it for your sake,
coming to enlace your neck, down hand over hand?
Our souls would blend as we made love on the forked highroad,
our mantles giving the cobbles a little heat.
So much for the unspoken contract whose fraudulent wording
the boisterous unhearing rain-wind has swept away!
As my eyes were going out did no one call after me?
If you had recalled me I'd have had one more day.
No watchman in my poor honour gave a rap with his cloven cane,
and my head, exposed, was gashed with a broken tile.
And did a single soul see you stooped at my grave in grief
or see your black toga grow hot with a stifled tear?
If you jibbed at going farther than up to my gate, at least
you might have seen the bier with less haste sent round.
Why did you, *you*, not petition the winds, thankless, for my tinder?
Why did *my* flames not emit aromatic spikenard?

Was this too much, to fling hyacinths, not exorbitant,
or propitiate my barrow from a spilt wine-jar?
And my serf Lygdamus: whiten the iron for him, cauterise him!
I knew from the wine when my blood went racing from it. . .
And let Nomas, sly as she is, hide her vials of arcane salivas!
The scorching pit she used then will point to her:
only lately in public eyed up and down through her cut-price nights,
and now marks the ground with a gold-inlaid modish hem;
who loads her bolshie maid with lumpier knitting baskets
if the jabberer has excessively praised my beauty.
And Petale—because she took a wreath to the cemetery,
the old thing gets fettered to a disgusting log.
Strung up by her writhing hair, Lalage's cut to pieces
because she dared mention me when she asked a favour;
and you gave her that gold statuette of me to be melted down,
and so she acquires a dowry from my cremation.
Yet I won't hound you, though you deserve it, Propertius, of me;
my despotic sovereignty in your verse was long.
I swear by the irreversible spell of the Fates, and may
the triple dog, for this, gentle its yelp around me,
I was always faithful to you. If I am lying then may
vipers hiss on my mound, make my bones their bed.
There are two haunts distributed by the ugly river
and all the riot dead must row either water;
one conveys the polluted Clytaemnestra, another carries
the freak timbers of the counterfeit Cretan cow.
But look, a garlanded sloop sweeps away yet another lot
where holy breezes caress the Elysian rose;
melodious strings and Cybele's circular cymbals bang
to the strum of the Lydian orchestra dressed in turbans.
Andromeda and Hypermestra, those stainless wives,
relate the events, notable souls, they suffered.
One moans of the maternal chains that have bruised her arms
and the glacial rocks her hands had not merited.
Hypermestra tells of her sisters' enormous daring
and how she had not the courage for such a crime.
And so with the tears of death we heal the desires of life;
I myself conceal your betrayals' atrocities.

48

But now I am giving you orders—if by chance you can be affected,
  if the herbs of Chloris have not yet seduced you wholly:
don't let my nurse, Parthene, go short when she's old and shaking;
  she put up with you, you never have found her greedy.
And don't let my darling Latris—her name's from *latreuein*—
  ['serve'—
extend the looking-glass for a new employer.
And all those poems you have written around my name,
  burn them for me, stop winning praise through me.
Push the ivy off of my mound, that amasses and struggles with
  its hairy twists bandaging my small bones apart.
And where fruit-bearing Anio communes with its branchy regions
  and Hercules sees that the ivory never yellows,
these lines, I am worthy of them, write square on a pillar, but
  make them, so the hurried commuter may read them, brief:
HERE LIES THE GOLDEN CYNTHIA IN THE FIELDS OF TIBUR:
  NOW FAME IS ADDED, ANIO, TO YOUR BANKS.
And do not reject apparitions coming through holy porches,
  when holy the apparition comes, it has weight.
By night we veer abroad, night loosens the pent-up ghost;
  even Cerberus goes vagrant, the bolts dismantled.
At dawn we make for the swamps, compelled by Lethean law;
  we sail; the ferryman catalogues his freight.
For now give yourself to others, soon I alone will have you,
  and mixed in the grave I'll grind you, bone on bone.'

When in this way she'd ended her querulous dispute with me,
  her spirit disappeared, my embrace was empty.

# Vox Dei

*Dearly beloved, I should like you to imagine for a while that these stones, these pillars of unweathered stone which get in the way when you want to see from the side, these flagstones too under which so many bones lie honoured in their long home, the stone vault which is a little nearer than heaven but not so cold sometimes, the threshold and lintel, the buttress and architrave, I want you to think that every complacent stone in this made shrine speaks, that every stone here speaks, and speaks to you. I want you to imagine that every stone of this fabrication speaks to you with the voice of God, that God speaks, and that he speaks to you from these stones, from the ancient elements, the calcium and silicon, in the masonry of this* sanctum sanctorum.

*He speaks from the crevice at your feet which may gullet and scuttle you into a nightmare of misgiving one day, but not now, it is not of your misgivings he speaks now with a voice as dry as a sleeper in the straw. He speaks from the rafter hole which would freeze your eye if you climbed that high because of the strips of cold air that have slid there from nowhere. He speaks to you from the draught near the* ont, *he exhales from the worn altar step, his breath labours from the flint founda-*tions.

*It is God's voice that speaks, the voice of the stone.*

Saying, 'Forgive me if I do not speak very clearly.'
Saying, 'I am sorry to intrude, to take up your time.'
Saying, 'It's my sore throat. I have a bad cold. Please forgive me.'
Saying, 'I am sorry you can hear me only in your head, and not in the air as you hear one another. I am sorry that you have to guess what I say. I am trying. I do not know where to start. I feel so humble. You speak so well and I do not have a language. You know things and I know nothing. What can I say? I am like a lover who would like to be noticed. I am like a parent who would like to be acknowledged. I am like a catastrophe that would like to be blamed. Man, without you I am catastrophic, a spank and rasping of particles inside an atom, a tornado of galaxies falling out with one another. Without you who can I please? Without you who can say I made anything? Without you who can curse me for my shortcomings? You do not have to listen to me, I know. You have a mind of your own. I have none.

'I have no mind. That is my trouble. I am not even out of my mind; that would be some consolation. For some time you thought I was brainy, that I could count, and so on. You thought I knew good from evil, that I had a degree in international law. I puzzled you. I don't wonder. Forgive me. It was not bright of me even to imply such powers. You found me out and were angry. You turned away.

'You have the mind. I do not even know that I am, as you do. Perhaps I am jealous. Yes, I am jealous of you. That's how it is. It made me act badly. You know all about yourself. You know about me and ignore me. Of course I am jealous, crazy. And there is always more you can know. Things are so vast, as you see them, so interesting, devious, odd.

'Odd! Not that I'm complaining, mind you. And I hesitate to say it since it may seem like boasting. And I'm sorry, truly, if you thought me vainglorious before. But odd it may seem all the same that the things you study are me. I mean, after all, everything existing is me. I say that without much pride. Truly. A humble submission, you might say. I am the crack in the floor and the hole in the rafter; I am the helium that aggregates in the sun, the oxygen that goes black in your lungs; I am the leaf that shies out before the sun thinks it fit, the cup that runs over; I am twenty-five million slaves and the gas chambers; I am natural selection and the law of diminishing returns; I am the girl on the beach and the war machine; I am so many stars that their number will change in the time it takes you to count them; I am the child's toy and the bread in the kitchen; I am the spectral waste in the water supply and the walk with friends; I am exceptional music and the idiot's slobber. You study these things, I know, you study—I am not complaining. You know all about me. I have no mind, how can I? I do not know where I am going or even if I began. I shall never be able to know it; you will, I am sure. You have so much I lack. You are aware.

'When the days come with the sun and the young rain again, tell me about them. Speak with the warmth going in you, put your tongue to the splash. What words would I like to hear? You are asking? I like you. You ask me. Say the sun is like a bridegroom coming out of his chamber. Say the tree by the river fruits in season like a man that is honest. Say a full table is a reminder of enemies. Say that central heating turns the arctic night inside out. Say the fox panting for the brook is like a man panting for the brook. Say the TV ad gives you the well-cooked meat of boredom. See into the crevices of your knowing; be honest with them.

51

Be more than honest, less than sincere, evasions are helpful. A walk in the street makes you happy and the walk back is deadly. A furtive love affair is like loving the stones. Say anything, I want to hear it. Meat on the Sabbath is better than ancient patricide. Is it not? Exaggerate for me. Please me. Notice the stones. How much of the dead moon stone is never noticed? How much of all there is can never be noticed? Notice me. Whatever you say you cannot make up for the stones that are never noticed.

'Imagine the stones were not. What numbers there are for your small seeing. Speak to me. Be proud of your insignificant eyes.

'What would the starfish be or the car bomb be without you? Speak to me. Say something unusual about them.

'Look at the tooth of the wasp, of the snail, of the shark. Are winter's teeth unkind? Speak of teeth, give me a casual example. Think of them with compassion: that is one way I hear; from your gut feeling.

'Let the murdered trunk on the embankment, as mere thing, as me, warm you as if you stood with the sculptor's David. Speak to me. I need you.

'Let the house of heartbroken shadows, as a mere thing, as me, warm you as if you were in a dark, lacy seashell. Speak to me. I need you.

'Let the beastliness of ancestral conventions, the ghosts that leave grease stains, as dead rituals, as mere things, as me, warm you as if you enjoyed an astonished infatuation. Speak to me.

'Let your fear of being nothing, a pushy filmset abandoned, a black terror, let your fear as a mere thing, as me, warm you as if you took coffee on a transcontinental journey. Speak to me, please.

'Let the arthritic claw in the marrow, famine after flood, loneliness growing in spite, roof gone or hankering to go, subtle passions made silly, let them, as mere things, as me, warm you as if you took wine. Speak to me. I am praying to you.

'I need you.

'I am only the stones. You must do the thinking for me. Say something.

'Speak.'

# Dead Serpentine

I watch at the fisherboy's shoulder.
He fishes the Serpentine. Fishes
for nothing. Nothing that I can see.
By the mid-afternoon his keepnet
is empty. My interest has grown lean.
Then he catches a nine-finned green thing
and lets it stand still in green nothing
as if the keepnet too were nothing.

The shore water is greasy. It has
matchsticks in it. Far out are sun-cups
and bronzed people in boats. And if those
bronzed people in boats could row me out
I would escape willingly. But here
like a mother-love silence before it rains
death means little to the fisherboy.

The skin of the shore flakes off and soaks.
The boy is the fish, the fish is dead,
a green banana, a submerged thumb.
He has fallen asleep under the green
like an old man. Tenderness of neck
turns to the tender sun. His dead hair
has clung to his chin. I am the boy.
I too can drown in desired nothing.

# Augury for Caesar

When you accede to the nightlong city
on seven hills, tired, to swallow days
that quail in a devouring calm,
your last years piled up on the marble slab
like satisfying, uncommon food—
if Fortune hold, as she has held, you'll find
late time warm in your veins
as foretimes were that wind back through earth's body
to your birth cry. The pillared city
will be your past, your memories well-seasoned.
And godlike it will mutter in you
before it is staled down to yellow water:
a history. That you created?
You? Remembering Pompey, bowelled to the heart
with guile's gravel, whom you gave
your daughter, toothsome naked, then the sharp
of your sword naked. Both of which
your soul gasped in. Recalling at Bithynia
(for Rome's good) you were 'queen', they said,
for capering in a saffron gown as one
to please a king at dinner. Remembering
great Crassus spied your horses given their head:
he studied you; you studied then
how the bit is slatted in a bloodier shout
when he nailed the slaves, six thousand, up
from Rome to Capua down the Appian Way.
Remembering your own head speak
in Further Spain by Alexander's statue:
stone by stone, a king calling.
Remembering your calling in Germania
when you had flogged to bone, among
his peers, a king, till he died. Remembering how
you wolfed back over the Rubicon
to drive Pompey to evacuate Rome,
dogging him to Alexandria

where your gorge sickened at the dead repast.
When godlike your bones fork these hills,
Julius Caesar, you may have bad dreams:
proconsul, imperator, rex:
how sage smelt in the dead camp morning; how women
smelt; consuming orgies; life
on a talent borrowed; the lower, strict field theory
of the bloodstream; the sinews' topographic
strain; campaigns; and the manship of campaign...
When late at night you walk in the still
city, reswallowing the past, repairing
to bed before the stars repair,
Caesar, galled god, your heartburn may say if
you made these days, these seething days,
or if each day the day was you, creator!
You may find, god, just what it is
you are. Before they flank the crown dish in:
Pompey's face in gravy on a platter
while your ship wallows off the Egyptian sands.

# Elektra

*for Kate Bush*

I   HER AGONY

*Time's steady state*

I've seen the leaf constrained to come
in summer, its foot glued to the bark,
hedged, sentenced to anonymous work,
buzz in hundreds, other times stay dumb.

An upright style stiffens the chronicler;
fashion ties the children to cocaine.
I've seen the dice, scarecrows in the rain,
and female suicides in mid-career.

I have heard voices stop at every turn
and faces ask, and if she tries
she can't escape those absolute eyes.
Summer closes in, the leaves have grown.

I've seen what time's steady state involves:
it prisons her; it gives her to the wolves.

*Grand'mere*

Usage is what she lives by, not a cage.
Who wants to be a prisoner all her life?
Who wants to live in a psychotic calm
upon the arm of a correct, stiff groom
that leads her doctor-like about his grounds?

Inside that towering, blackened, lakeside schloss
she listens to her dark, a gramophone
slurring: 'Although *(whirr)* apart you know *(whirr)*
my heart's *(whirr)*-ing for you.' There's no escape
from the acoustics of inbred despair.

And he will lead her sometimes, if he cares,
out to the pink and grey, imperial square,
a montagne music frozen under the bandstand's
twiddly baldacchino. How long ago did she lose
courage? In how many punctilious gardens?

He is correct and honest and studies birds
and lives on a prohibitively high opinion
of her and of himself. Years long she studied him.
Now he conducts her bones in a wheelchair.
Her daughter will topple a statue and squash them flat.


*The god of the woods*

His laugh no refuge, the safe
doctor so many lies,
his bones squeaking, an aged
resentment in his eyes,

the god of the wood ushers
the young girl to her chair,
she falters: 'You are changing.'
And fear fringes her hair.

'Little patient,' he answers,
'the enduring face will win.
I have shed a hundred masks.
Your peeling off begins.'


*Her fashion now*                              .

He is the victim, speaks for a perished species:
it cannot be that he will have long life.
She ties him down. The work done in her field
is the difference between their two potentials:
his fossil past, her flight to yet-to-be.

Wired for feeling, her batteries of change
charge her electrons through him. And she flows.
She orchestrates his pain: jocose vibrato.
And makes him her conductor: let him feel
*her* insert finger and *her* right-hand rule.

She'll worship him no more—this Stephano?
God of the isle? Or of the jungle city?
This ghastly Tlaloc, lord of mountains and maize
that they cooked babies for? She ties him down.
Opens his heart and lets the sewer out.

His system's poisoned by his remedies,
but her great switch is thrown. Her quick volcano,
rivelled, pursed up, from its electric core
ejects, and on her slopes grow oranges.
It is her fashion now—his *dernier cri*.


58

*Elektra*

Fey, unoriginal, refracting
quotations from belittled canzoni,
she is drawn to those unlike her.
Among the derivatives of *fin-de-siècle*
she chooses the stroller with the black malacco.

Then see her at evening, aromatic dance,
as sticky as grenadine, as orange,
a secular variation of Earth's field,
her nipples exchanging kill-crackle,
her navel the white spot that roves on Jupiter.

She touches what she will, turns it on;
gives the pagoda a banal appearance;
leaves the stroller mystified; steals his cane.
Come dawn, her magnetic flux, like a cat,
waits for the milkman, his cold crates.

*Who goes*

Who goes in the electric wind, vibrating,
who seeks a share in it, lost dreams,
who has her elements on the money,
who finds less limitation in the cold,
who goes back twenty years to a *café chantant*,

who remembers his frosty eyes, sandpipers,
who goes without certain home,
who does not correct herself, but alters,
who stayed three weeks and disturbed a legend,
who pretends to read on a bad afternoon,

who lies in a mummy case, a parched river,
who candies the twigs with frost in autumn,
who has UFO eyes and a black halo,
who gave the saint his incredible eyes,
who enters the acid, covers the plate with silver.


*She flies*

The stars are as they are by accident.
His time is little to their outward speed.
A tree is nearer to him, and it feels
less than he does, maybe, but more than she.

She sees no reason why she should not leave—
and that's the story of his life, or hers?
Whose outward urge, or inner spin, is more
in conflict with relentless gravity?

The padlocked atom, the domestic core
was murdered from her at her birth: she flies
to outswim all the tadpole galaxies
and taste the frontier of the brittle dark.

Outstripping, stripped, her force will not exist
and from the tree the last pale leaf will fall
that kept the tree in motion. He may touch
his tree, her dark, then die, and that is all.

*Isis*

And now the rain is beginning, and she is
all about us. She is in love still.
Gutters run pure. Although she can rip trees,
drown valleys, she is gentle this evening.

Her moon burns by the twig in the pool,
like an eye's burning, hard, honest
The hills are, like horizon hills,
a country we may never come to.

Her rain is measuring itself around us,
and that is her way: the shaken water
and two hollows, our shapes exactly.
The gods can hurt. When they do not we are grateful.


*The moonstone*

I will have no more fiction. She is
the moonstone on the bed of the pool,
the transmuting eye in the psyche,
the one drop of dew drowned under air,
the coin in the child's jar, forgotten,
for decades forgotten, but seen now.

I am tired of all these lies. She is
the mouth in the bone cell that eats me,
the botfly that grubs in my vitals,
the ever rain, the wet in the stone,
the architecture's impediment,
the quick smile that will bring the house down.

These are the facts, these only. I am
in charge of my passionate terrors.
I have trawled in her sea-change. I have
extirpated the guilt in the cell.
She is being's bride, and non-being's.
She looks up at me. The night trembles.

I am tired of creation's deceits,
that blood is red, the stars beyond me,
and that my dust is uncountable.
There is only one thing. It is she.
The hermetic eye. I plunge my arm
into the water. I grip my side.

Envoi

*Where are the girls of yesteryear*

Where are the girls of yesteryear
who have illuminated me?
    Where Sue Strap with the college eyes,
    where Madame Krabb, the doyenne of spies,
    where the pilafs of Edith Gear,
Joan Hasitwell and grave Marie,
Violet Hyssop, Dol Dare, oh where?
    I was briefly conscious of what you were.
    *What happens to electricity?*

Where are the girls of yesteryear
who rang my brain from ear to ear?
　Where Moll Flanders, the clever dear,
　where Griselda's uninjured air,
　where Florence (her swabs were regular),

Nell Gwyn, soft-centred Marjorie,
M. Curie and Eva Braun, oh where?
　You rode the footlights, caused a stir.
　*What happens to electricity?*

Where are the girls of yesteryear
who ran me round with coils of hair?
　Where Joy, who's in Holloway still,
　where La Gioconda, whose frown could kill,
　where Anne Frank in her attic lair,
Hedda, Blanche, Eurydice,
Fiona Fitz-Pussy in boots, oh where?
　You curled along my wire, bare.
　*What happens to electricity?*

Where are the girls of yesteryear
who are beyond telepathy?
　Where Keller, who heard what she saw,
　where the Dickens, that brood she bore,
　where Jane's tongue that I used to hear,
Never-Titty, starved Emily,
Medea and Albertine, oh where?
　You are white noise in the atmosphere.
　*What happens to electricity?*

# For Lady Moon

Considering how euphoria has failed,
hit a main line of remorse
and open a new chapter of romantic history.
Hang decals in your hair:
serenity, tranquillity, pumpkin seed.
Refuse to plead guilty that you blew your cool
and put out garbage everyone else kept in.
Do your damnedest, blast your way to hell;
walk where the rain slices the dawn;
change the shape of a stony tear in water
and see where the bridge breaks.
    Keep alive her bright image everywhere.

Considering how money chokes its world,
spend a lifetime on a stone linear
of CIA instructions.
See how many men of judgment
you can despise for any reason.
See the eyes of mistrust and refuse
to wear them even as a badge of honour.
Keep paranoia like a cat for spiteful occasions.
A night jeep patrols the black oilwells
like a beetle in the sky's rat skull.
Look with melancholy at the frittered luggage
of passengers shot down in the sand.
    But keep alive her bright image everywhere.

Considering how the city is not home,
live in it all the same, fouled asteroid,
where high blocks bite the eye
like lasers, and where envoys die.
Things must have a place to happen in.
The ungovernable must sow their seed and thrive.
You cannot be sure where your ego goes—
allow for it a little,

it hasn't murdered anyone for weeks,
allow a little for the unsatisfied.
 Keep alive her bright image everywhere.

Considering that Eros is defiled,
give a party, first in years,
and outrage your newest friends.
Develop a protective pride
for your libidinous failings.
Match your deathwish with almost everybody's
idea of bad theatre.
Let the party sag on till three in the morning,
what time the venery will leave
into a winter air like paint remover.
Grow young as your better half
psychs out with a few contentment hobbies.
 But keep alive her bright image everywhere.

It does not matter that good feeling fails;
any empire chokes, money or no;
cities were always better for the few;
love never cared, it doesn't have to care.
 Keep alive her image. Everywhere.

# An Age Turns

Highwind at Whitsuntide and all week
living is an aftermath: I haul
its ashes. I never requested
an out from the steep ducts of feeling.
All knowledge is carnal, no cause lasts
sixty years, a sealed wine dries. Nature,
they say your beauty is in my mind.
Come the next City they will dispense
with us entirely, both. If I had
a pistol I would oil it ten times
daily. Outside, spits of dull spring rain
in the ear, the petals from the crux
of the tulip snap, and the greenhouse
can do without me. I have brought home
some Chinese food, our privet has worms,
and I am designing a doorway
against intrusion, a monk's cell, lit
by a Mazda WAM pendant. It seems
the hottest day is never the year's
lightest day. I have no heat either.
Mozart reinterprets the grand scale
and I am not sure I am happy
if in some way his buffos touch parts
of the sempiternal. Apes see more
than they need, reflections in water
and the Aurora Borealis.
My mother is propped in the toolshed
with a cobweb of lace and brocades.
My daughter writes crap for a part-work
on Freud, finding herself with old men
and despair. They have leached the colour
from family reserves. She looks bad.
The antique perspectives are staved in,
a bombed-out cathedral. I would like
a village just recently streetcleaned

by summer rain, a place into which
all distances hankered and ended;
where the cockerel at morning would pull
its cry out of three mildewed klaxons
with no hint of churches or torment;
where fauns every day would copulate
among the beeches and cool bluebells;
where no one played significant games
like stud, patience, or consequences.
It's a shame Brunelleschi's stoa
survives as a blueprint to vex me:
a simple arcade to walk round in.
Even in my youth I was turned on
by ruins—which is wrong—the grass keep
and the shattered staircase, the corners,
open-air and forbidden, the dark
inside. Ossian, Beethoven, Turner
started the disease, and all that fall
from night thoughts to end-tapes in dustbins.
There's a flat after-century taste
in my marrow bones. The dislodged world
rolls from God's hand like a crucifix
from a man's hand dying. God is not
dead: he may be not-yet, or nothing,
though our own god, man's, may be over,
drugged, dragged and dredged out of Israel.
What's this that it is mindful? All grass
invades. My summerhouse has decayed.
It's cloudy. The sun's our nearest star.
If music heals, recomposes, what
surgery will follow this moist day—
my life's undiagnosable smear?
A book is a cemetery, Proust
averred, and begged no questions on love.
Which, I suppose—love—can be reckoned
to muffle in my veins too like hoarse
discontinuous rales of thunder
trapped in time, shocks which carried me through

many unsustained selves, sustaining
my affair with things. It is children
I recall most, though this pugging wind
scuttles them into coigns of my mind
deprived and fed by sea-cows. Shadows.
Love rather overwhelms me. A sort
of necessary empire, killer
of its grovelling and great, blurred
template of such things as law and chance,
(form in chaos, purposes in void?)
*in me tota ruens:* Phaedra's love,
or like the antibiotics of
Jesus, it ruins, it chokes me, like
Schönberg from the Bluthner Boudoir grand
or flowers in my vase by Scabra.
I renounce love, if love will let me.
My skull dates, from carbon half-life loss,
between Tiberius and the last
Sinn Fein dynasty in Uganda.
A name like Faust or Foster. My cat
gets its eyes from Karnak. A new god
has monopoly of circumstance.

# All Dead But

I can say what it is like to be carrion,
to be digested alive until I am half alive,
to be like a fly held in the crippled elbow
of a praying mantis which nibbles, nibbles
my bowels like so much whipped ice-cream:

to be like a wild dog on the ruthless plain
lame and behind the pack which entrusts me
to the mean teeth of a diligent hyena.
Fear wobbles my every gland, my each heartbeat
has seized upon too much time and all of it wasted.

I can talk of this because a woman eats me
with her inattentive pity, her copybook smiles,
her frank worthlessness, her cold assurance.
I am numbly near to being god-kissed remains.
I too have dined this way. It is usual now.

# Gone

When the light's gone from our eyes, and loneliness
is better company at night than bed;
when booze depresses, and a few grey hairs
are all I need to think of menopause;

when the drive to work along back winter streets
where suburbs have been emptied for the day
of family heat and love's economies
never lasts long enough to lead back where

we were on holiday always and we smiled;
when—when self-pity is corroding me
and friends are kept away as if they scald;
when the worst is time to come, the time which holds

the children gone, and me with little pride,
I have thought of my father, whose joys were few,
('When you two boys were young,' he says) and thought
there might be yet some swinish pleasure left

in sucking dry the common tits of woe:
I'm of an age when there's a choice—do I
wish all the best to love, and bare a smile,
or envy the dead heart, learn its reserves?

# Our Gerbil, Dead

It was such a little thing
in our lives, out of the way
on the kids' bedroom table,
apparently contented
with a lifetime's dull diet
of water, hamster biscuit
and central heating's seasons.
He had his own looking glass,
a treadmill, and one eggbox
a day to chew to small bits
for exercise in nesting.
We never gave him a mate
because, we knew, prisoners
like him, from birth, would savage
anything like a trial
friend of his own kind put in.
He knew only divine love,
ours; lesser he did not trust.
He'd not run far from his cage
when allowed out; accepted
his minute infinity
shyly; never knew the world
gerbils are supposed to know.

Now he is dead. For one night
he lay, eyes shut, shivering
in the grip of last decay.
We laid him in a kingsize
economy 'Ship' matchbox
lined with dress material.
Undine cried. Crispin sniggered.
I dug him a grave outside
the door. And my little thought
tried to reach out to Lise
sleepless beside her mother

dying of liver cancer,
and now to my own mother
dying, by coincidence,
as well, as well of cancer.
They'd had their hour with the glass.
Both did daily their house chores.
Both would have quelled the first sign
of an unfamiliar
human advance. Both kept close
to home. Both had singular
trust in the droppers of food
and carriers of cages.
Neither, shivering her last,
would think it her right to cry,
wail, unanimal, 'My God,
why have you forsaken me?'

I go too about my work
heavy with death, with no sense,
no right, to feel forsaken.

# Death's Head

At least I was lucky. I managed
to mourn you, mother.
In spite of the corpses frozen
on the lower bunks of the Gulag trains.

I stood at your feet crying,
your frail death's head,
shrunken, historical,
stone or wax to my kiss.
From these bones I came.
And I felt so guilty towards you.

Not everyone is so lucky
with tears to exorcise guilt,
to have the dust signal in silence
that he is forgiven, he must go.

How many were deprived by those trains
under the soap clouds of corpse smoke
hung round the earth as it veered
into this century?
With all those bodies heaped like a ghastly mistake
how many millions in the done-up cities
were able to put their lips
to an identified head?

# Winter Transit

Snow dots printed on the cold;
a puffed-up robin on a fence;
the far garden wild with old
vegetable irrelevance;

a move inside the barren twigs
as bird bolts in then leaves be
a springing of little spars and rigs
on a sea bottom drained of sea;

a whiteness on the silent green
of yew in which two squirrels run;
a clothes line under which, clean,
hangs an empty phenomenon;

such is the time, such the day
for you, friend, at your last hold,
condemned, this wintertime your way
through terminal disease to cold.

Such is the land of in between
in which our ghost, projected, words
the timeless yew and ivy's green:
no life, no sound, except of birds:

a doing-nothing ghost, unless
it tremble in the nothing, far
into the white wild, and cannot guess
that boys ganged in the pergola.

One day birds die. And night falls.
White disappears in a black rain.
No ghost. A bruised blur first. Then all's
a perfect black that will remain,

remain for a numb eternity
for our poor melted ghost. Spring will
bud, June fuse, autumn's debris
confuse with nostalgias, and thrill.

New birds will come. But under the leaves
the bones that wait will wait in vain.
No voice of ours will quick them. Grieves
the heart. It may do. Come again

the heart will not. Threading the boughs
other birds, boys, there will be. One
may feel as we do: a mind may house
thoughts that through our life have run.

We contemplate the cold. What must
be left we'll leave. Here is the fence
on which the snow builds; here is the crust
the birds peck for last sustenance.

Snow dots and prints upon the cold
clear air that works upon our world.
A wild bird shifts its wild song, doled
from a dark hole, at the darkness hurled.

# Cat Woman

Cats exercised in the garage. Cats
kept in cages along the walls.
Her old double mattress pads the door.
Keeps the locals insensible.

Once a week she berates the grumble-guts
who rents from her a slum by the arch.
Wants him out. Could sell to a builder.
Man mumbles: his son says he stinks.

On the waste ground between the old arch
and the strip of motorway beyond
she chats up boys. Do they break windows?
But they do nothing. Nor does she.

Till she is visited by a daughter. Who sniffs
at the houseplants. Dusty. Who wants money
for her sister on the game in Soho,
hooked by heroin on a gutter dream.

What's she to me? says the cat woman.
What are my fine daughters to me?
Then: out of hours to the old man's.
An awful night. Picks up stones,

detonates all his windows, lets
his oil-fire oil drain from the drum
at his kitchen door. Home through the ache
of the outer city's coldest wind.

A month: the man gone. A cheque
makes its way to her addict daughter.
But the cats pay. Two are set to fight
till their ears rip and one's made blind.

# Lullaby

to the edge of my bed a tone
  fine and corrupted came
from the dark fringe of my home
  from the dark outside the room

as long as anything was
  the dark has been growing there
in the yard where those relics lodge
  that the head can no longer store

brains harden into dust
  in a junk-yard in a void
where the fine and the corrupt
  are huddled and ignored

all our time is for now
  intones the mothering air
memory measures us out
  and then we disappear